STATES

NEW YORK

A MyReportLinks.com Book

Corinne J. Naden
and Rose Blue

MyReportLinks.com Books
an imprint of
Enslow Publishers, Inc.
Box 398, 40 Industrial Road
Berkeley Heights, NJ 07922
USA

MyReportLinks.com Books, an imprint of Enslow Publishers, Inc.

Library of Congress Cataloging-in-Publication Data

Naden, Corinne J.
  New York / Corinne J. Naden & Rose Blue.
     p. cm. — (States)
Includes bibliographical references and index.
Summary: Discusses the land and climate, economy, government, and
history of the state of New York.
  ISBN 0-7660-5016-5
  1. New York (State)—Juvenile literature. [1. New York (State)] I.
Blue, Rose. II. Title. III. States (Series : Berkeley Heights, N.J.)
  F119.3 .N34 2002
  974.7—dc21
                                    2001004313

Printed in the United States of America

10 9 8 7 6 5 4 3 2 1

To Our Readers:
Through the purchase of this book, you and your library gain access to the Report Links that specifically back up this book.
The Publisher will provide access to the Report Links that back up this book and will keep these Report Links up to date on **www.myreportlinks.com** for three years from the book's first publication date.
We have done our best to make sure all Internet addresses in this book were active and appropriate when we went to press. However, the author and the Publisher have no control over, and assume no liability for, the material available on those Internet sites or on other Web sites they may link to.
The usage of the MyReportLinks.com Books Web site is subject to the terms and conditions stated on the Usage Policy Statement on **www.myreportlinks.com.**
In the future, a password may be required to access the Report Links that back up this book. The password is found on the bottom of page 4 of this book.
Any comments or suggestions can be sent by e-mail to comments@myreportlinks.com or to the address on the back cover.

Photo Credits: AP Photo/Graham Morrison, p. 43; © Corel Corporation, pp. 3, 10, 11, 27, 29, 43; Courtesy of LongIslandHistory.com, pp. 34, 36; Courtesy of MyReportLinks.com Books, p. 4; Courtesy of The Catskill Guide, p. 21; Courtesy of The City of Buffalo, p. 22; Courtesy of The National Baseball Hall of Fame and Museum, p. 14; Courtesy of The New York State Assembly, p. 31; Courtesy of The New York Times on the Web, p. 40; Courtesy of The Saratoga County Chamber of Commerce, p. 38; Courtesy of The United States Military Academy, p. 19; Courtesy of The Western New York Railroad Archive, p. 26; Courtesy of WNET/ Thirteen, PBS, pp. 12, 41; Enslow Publishers, Inc., pp. 1, 17; Joseph Migliacci, DVM, p. 18; The Library of Congress, pp. 3 (Constitution), 16.

Cover photo: © Corel Corporation.

Contents

MyReportLinks.com Books
Great Books, Great Links, Great for Research!

MyReportLinks.com Books present the information you need to learn about your report subject. In addition, they show you where to go on the Internet for more information. The pre-evaluated Report Links that back up this book are kept up to date on **www.myreportlinks.com**. With the purchase of a MyReportLinks.com Books title, you and your library gain access to the Report Links that specifically back up that book. The Report Links save hours of research time and link to dozens—even hundreds—of Web sites, source documents, and photos related to your report topic.

Please see "To Our Readers" on the Copyright page for important information about this book, the MyReportLinks.com Books Web site, and the Report Links that back up this book.

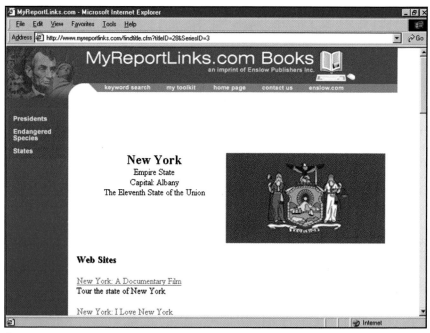

Access:

The Publisher will provide access to the Report Links that back up this book and will try to keep these Report Links up to date on our Web site for three years from the book's first publication date. Please enter **SNY1224** if asked for a password.

Report Links

The Internet sites described below can be accessed at
http://www.myreportlinks.com

*EDITOR'S CHOICE

▶**New York: A Documentary Film**
At this Web site you can take a virtual tour of New York City's five
boroughs, where you will learn about some of the city's interesting
historical attractions.

Link to this Internet site from http://www.myreportlinks.com

*EDITOR'S CHOICE

▶**New York: I Love New York**
This site provides facts and figures on the state of New York. Here you
will find the state flag, state symbol, a list of famous New Yorkers, and
other facts and statistical information.

Link to this Internet site from http://www.myreportlinks.com

*EDITOR'S CHOICE

▶**Ellis Island**
At this Web site you can explore the history of Ellis Island, where 22
million immigrants entered the United States between 1892 and 1924.

Link to this Internet site from http://www.myreportlinks.com

*EDITOR'S CHOICE

▶**New York State**
At this site you can explore New York parks, recreation sites, and
historical places. You will also learn about New York's governor and
New York state government.

Link to this Internet site from http://www.myreportlinks.com

*EDITOR'S CHOICE

▶**Get the Facts About New York**
This Web site provides an overview of New York's history from 1524 to
the present. You will also find New York's state symbols, the origin of
county names, a list of New York governors, and fun related games.

Link to this Internet site from http://www.myreportlinks.com

*EDITOR'S CHOICE

▶**One Hundred Years of New York City**
At this Web site you can explore the past one hundred years of New
York City's history. Here you will find a collection of articles, essays,
and poems offering a glimpse into New York City's past, as well as
images reflecting the times.

Link to this Internet site from http://www.myreportlinks.com

The Internet sites described below can be accessed at
http://www.myreportlinks.com

▶**The American Presidency: Millard Fillmore**
Millard Fillmore was one of four native New Yorkers to become president of
the United States. At this site you will learn about Fillmore's political career
and life during his presidency.

Link to this Internet site from http://www.myreportlinks.com

▶**Empire State Building**
At this Web site you can take a tour of the Empire State Building, where
you will learn about the building's history, find facts and trivia, and
view photographs.

Link to this Internet site from http://www.myreportlinks.com

▶**Grain Elevators: A History**
At this Web site you will learn about grain elevators, which were an
important industry in Buffalo.

Link to this Internet site from http://www.myreportlinks.com

▶**The Battle of Saratoga**
This site includes details of the Revolutionary War battles that took place
near Saratoga, New York, and provides a look at reenactments of the battles
from both the American and British sides.

Link to this Internet site from http://www.myreportlinks.com

▶**Henry Hudson**
America's Story from America's Library, a Library of Congress Web site,
features an overview of Henry Hudson, the English explorer for whom the
Hudson River is named.

Link to this Internet site from http://www.myreportlinks.com

▶**Long Island: Our Story**
This Web site provides a comprehensive history of Long Island. Here
you will learn everything from Long Island's early days to its suburban
development. You will also find family stories, time lines, and a vault of
Long Island treasures.

Link to this Internet site from http://www.myreportlinks.com

Report Links

The Internet sites described below can be accessed at http://www.myreportlinks.com

▶ **Lower East Side Tenement Museum**

At this Web site you will learn about the history of tenement housing in New York City. Here you can take a virtual tour of the buildings and learn about the people who lived in them.

Link to this Internet site from http://www.myreportlinks.com

▶ **The City of Buffalo**

This Web site for the city of Buffalo offers facts and figures about New York's second largest city as well as interactive maps of the city and surrounding area.

Link to this Internet site from http://www.myreportlinks.com

▶ **The Metropolitan Museum of Art**

At the Metropolitan Museum of Art in New York City, you can take a virtual tour of the museum's collections. Here you will find everything from medieval to modern art, rare books, costumes, and much more.

Link to this Internet site from http://www.myreportlinks.com

▶ **The Museum of Modern Art**

At the Web site of the Museum of Modern Art in New York City, you can explore some of the museum's collections. You will learn about modern architecture, design, painting, photography, and much more.

Link to this Internet site from http://www.myreportlinks.com

▶ **The National Baseball Hall of Fame and Museum**

Located in Cooperstown, New York, is the National Baseball Hall of Fame and Museum. Here you can learn about baseball's legacy in American culture.

Link to this Internet site from http://www.myreportlinks.com

▶ **New York City's Gracie Mansion**

This site provides a brief history of Gracie Mansion. You will also learn about the New York City mayors who have lived in the mansion.

Link to this Internet site from http://www.myreportlinks.com

Report Links

The Internet sites described below can be accessed at
http://www.myreportlinks.com

▶New York Kids

This Web site, designed specifically for kids in New York City, is a companion to the *New York Kids* radio broadcast from WNYC. Here you will find educational games all about New York.

Link to this Internet site from http://www.myreportlinks.com

▶New York Underground

By navigating through this site, you can take a virtual tour of New York's underground. Here you can explore the underground transportation systems, sewage, geology, and myths surrounding the world underneath the city.

Link to this Internet site from http://www.myreportlinks.com

▶Niagara: A History of the Falls

At this Web site you will discover the history of Niagara Falls and find stories of individuals who rode over the falls in barrels.

Link to this Internet site from http://www.myreportlinks.com

▶West Point

The Web site for the United States Military Academy includes information about the academy's history and why its location on the banks of the Hudson River makes it an important fort even today. West Point has been training cadets since 1802.

Link to this Internet site from http://www.myreportlinks.com

▶Online Guide to the Catskill Mountains

At this Web site you will find photographs, online books, and essays related to the Catskills. You will also learn about some of the famous people who have lived there.

Link to this Internet site from http://www.myreportlinks.com

▶The Presidents: FDR

This Web site provides a comprehensive overview of Franklin Delano Roosevelt, a native New Yorker and United States president. Here you will learn about his early career, politics, and legacy.

Link to this Internet site from http://www.myreportlinks.com

Report Links

The Internet sites described below can be accessed at
http://www.myreportlinks.com

▶**The Skyscraper Museum**
By taking a virtual tour through the Skyscraper Museum, you will learn
about the history and architecture of many New York buildings.

Link to this Internet site from http://www.myreportlinks.com

▶**South Street Seaport Museum**
At the South Street Seaport Museum you will learn about some of the
nation's largest sailing vessels and the history of South Street Seaport.

Link to this Internet site from http://www.myreportlinks.com

▶**Tesla: Life and Legacy**
By navigating through this Web site, you will learn about Nikola Tesla
and his contributions toward the transmission of hydroelectric energy
from Niagara Falls to greater New York. You can also take a virtual tour
to learn how hydroelectric power works.

Link to this Internet site from http://www.myreportlinks.com

▶**Theodore Roosevelt Association**
At this Web site you can explore the life and legacy of Theodore
Roosevelt, a native New Yorker and the twenty-sixth president of the
United States.

Link to this Internet site from http://www.myreportlinks.com

▶**A Walk Around Brooklyn**
This Web site provides a comprehensive history of Brooklyn, New
York. Here you will find interactive maps that take you to many
Brooklyn neighborhoods and links to other resources.

Link to this Internet site from http://www.myreportlinks.com

▶**Western New York Railroad Archives**
At this site you can learn all about the railroads in western New York.
This site provides the history of the many major railroads that operated
in New York.

Link to this Internet site from http://www.myreportlinks.com

▶ **Capital**
Albany

▶ **Population**
18,976,457*

▶ **Bird**
Bluebird

▶ **Tree**
Sugar maple

▶ **Flower**
Rose

▶ **Animal**
Beaver

▶ **Fish**
Brook trout

▶ **Insect**
Nine-spotted lady beetle

▶ **Fruit**
Apple

▶ **Gemstone**
Garnet

▶ **Song**
"I Love New York," words
and music by Steve Karmen

▶ **Motto**
Excelsior, "Ever Upward"

▶ **Flag**
Dark blue with state coat
of arms in center showing
ships on a river, mountains,
and a rising sun; figures
representing Liberty and
Justice; and state motto.

▶ **Nickname**
The Empire State

Population reflects the 2000 census.

Chapter 1 ▶

The State of New York

It is thought that New York's nickname, the Empire State, has its origins with George Washington. In one of his visits to the state, in 1783, he is supposed to have predicted that New York would become the "seat of an empire." New York, one of the thirteen original colonies, played a pivotal role in the Revolutionary War. And the state's largest city, New York City, served as the nation's capital from 1785 to 1790. Today, New York's population of 18,976,457 (2000 U.S. census) makes New York the third largest state in population, behind California and Texas. New Yorkers go to the theater on Broadway. They watch the horses run at Saratoga Springs. They visit spectacular Niagara Falls. They tour General George Washington's head-quarters in Newburgh. They live and

The Statue of Liberty, which has stood ▶ in New York Harbor since 1886, has been the first sight of America for many immigrants to the United States.

work in fertile farmlands and bustling cities. And 8,008,278 of them live in the state's largest—and most famous—city, New York City.

▶ The Big Apple

Considered one of the world's greatest cities, New York City is a place like no other. Its population is one of the most diverse in the world. It is renowned as a center of finance, fashion, publishing, advertising, entertainment, and international politics. To many, New York City is the

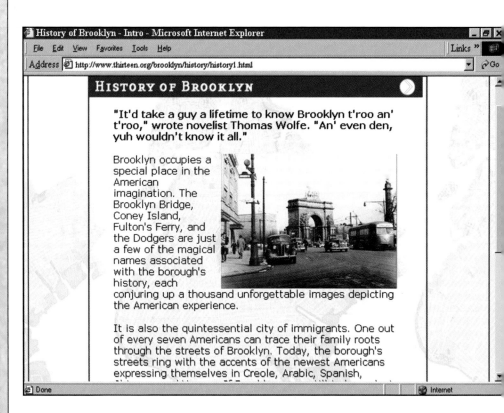

▲ One of New York City's five boroughs, Brooklyn is the home to many diverse neighborhoods where accents from the Middle East, Latin America, Asia, and nearly every other region on earth can be found on the borough's streets.

"Big Apple." That nickname comes from John J. FitzGerald, a reporter who coined the name in the 1920s to speak of the city's racetracks. In the 1930s, jazz musicians used it to describe New York as the jazz capital of the world, since "apple" was a slang term for "city."

The city is made up of five boroughs: Manhattan, Brooklyn, Queens, the Bronx, and Staten Island. Only the Bronx, named for Jonas Bronck, who owned the land in 1639, is part of the mainland. The other boroughs are islands connected by bridges and tunnels. Though Manhattan is the smallest in area of the five, it contains the landmarks of the city that people all over the world recognize—the United Nations Building, the bright lights of Broadway, the city waterfront, and the world-famous skyline of skyscrapers. One of the most easily recognized skyscrapers is the Empire State Building. Completed in 1931, in the depths of the Depression, the 102-story building was a remarkable engineering feat for its time. It remains one of the most popular tourist destinations for visitors to New York City.

▶ Other Attractions: Falls and Halls

The Empire State, however, has attractions beyond those of New York City. Tucked away in the far northwestern tip, on the border with Ontario, Canada, is spectacular Niagara Falls, on the Niagara River north of Buffalo. The falls spill 40 million gallons of water a minute as they drop over a ledge that is 180 feet high and two thirds of a mile wide. One of the most impressive natural wonders of North America, Niagara Falls attracts more than 10 million visitors each year.[1]

New York is also home to many halls of fame. One of the best known is the National Baseball Hall of Fame and

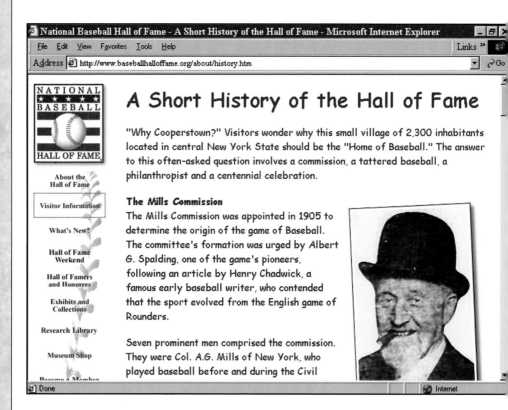

▲ In central New York, the village of Cooperstown is home to one of the most famous sports shrines in the world—the National Baseball Hall of Fame and Museum.

Museum, in Cooperstown. Opened in 1939, the Baseball Hall of Fame features baseball memorabilia and plaques of each player inducted into the hall. There are eighteen other halls of fame in the state, including one for maple syrup, in Crogan; one for fly fishing, in Livingston Manor; and one honoring great women, in Seneca Falls, the site of the first women's rights convention, in 1848. New York even has a hall of fame whose name sounds as if it displays dirt! Actually, the DIRT Hall of Fame Museum in Cayuga County features a collection of race cars and honors the legends of dirt-track racing.

Nature and Culture

New York is a place for outdoor recreation, too. In winter, skiers flock to trails in the Catskill and Adirondack Mountains. In autumn, spectacular foliage and breathtaking hiking and biking trails draw many visitors. There are more than 2,000 miles of hiking trails in the state. In summer, swimmers can find relief in the ocean along New York's 127 miles of Atlantic coastline. And there are thousands of lakes and ponds for swimming, boating, and fishing.

Music can be found nearly everywhere in the Empire State. New York City is home to Lincoln Center for the Performing Arts—the largest cultural complex in the world.[2] Lincoln Center is the site of the Metropolitan Opera House, the Julliard School, and the New York Philharmonic, among other famous venues. Radio City Music Hall, in New York City's Rockefeller Center, hosts the famous high-kicking Rockettes. Most people recognize these dancers from the nationally televised Macy's Thanksgiving Day Parade. There is plenty of music to be found outside of the city, too. The Peaceful Valley Bluegrass Festival in the Catskills, the Bayou Blues and Music Festival in the Hudson Valley, the Summer Fiddle Jamboree in the Adirondacks, and the New York State Rhythm and Blues Festival in Syracuse are just some of the music festivals held in the Empire State.

Native Sons and Presidents

Four United States presidents were born in New York. Martin Van Buren, the eighth president, was born in Kinderhook and is buried there. Millard Fillmore, the thirteenth president, was born in Cayuga County and is buried in Buffalo. Theodore Roosevelt, the twenty-sixth

president, was born in New York City and is buried at Oyster Bay on Long Island. His home, Sagamore Hill, is a national historic site. Theodore Roosevelt's distant cousin, Franklin Delano Roosevelt, the thirty-second president, was born in Dutchess County at the family estate of Hyde Park. Like Sagamore Hill, Hyde Park is also a national historic site. FDR's library, open to the public, contains more than thirty thousand books as well as the president's papers and memorabilia.

Both Theodore Roosevelt (top) and Franklin Delano Roosevelt (bottom) were born in New York, served as governor of the state, and went on to become United States presidents. Their homes in Oyster Bay, Long Island, and Hyde Park are national historic sites.

Land and Climate

New York has an area of 47,224 square miles.[1] Its length east to west covers 440 miles, including Long Island. Lake Ontario and the Canadian provinces of Ontario and Quebec form New York's northern border. Lake Champlain, Vermont, Massachusetts, Connecticut, and the Atlantic Ocean are to the east. To the south are New

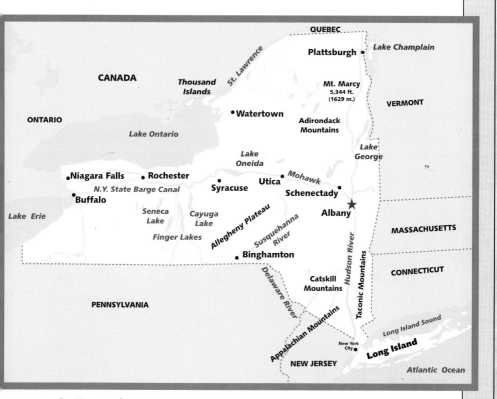

▲ New York.

▲ *A hiker's efforts are rewarded with a breathtaking view of the Adirondack Mountains.*

Jersey and Pennsylvania, and Lake Erie is to the west. Long Island is at the southeastern tip of the state.

▶ Eleven Regions

New York can be divided into eleven regions. The *Thousand Islands-Seaway* region runs along Lake Ontario and the St. Lawrence River. This majestic waterway stretches some 2,500 miles from Minnesota until it empties into the Gulf of St. Lawrence in Canada. In this region, the river is dotted with almost two thousand islands. It is a place of marvelous scenery, historic forts, and many art museums.

The *Adirondacks* region occupies a large part of the state's mountainous northeast. The Adirondack Mountains are named after an American Indian tribe that once inhabited the region. The Adirondacks are an old mountain chain, perhaps America's oldest. Its peaks have been worn down by the centuries into rounded tops and deep gorges. The highest peak in the region, and in the state, is Mount

Marcy, at 5,344 feet. The Adirondacks are covered with maples, oaks, and evergreens. Thousands of ponds and lakes can be found here, so it is easy to see why the region is known for its hiking trails, swimming, and fishing.

South of the Adirondacks is the *Capital-Saratoga* region. Albany, the state capital, is found here. So is Saratoga Springs, known for mineral baths and horse racing. Much of this region is rural and features covered bridges and quaint villages settled hundreds of years ago.

The *Hudson Valley* region, named for the area surrounding the state's largest river, can be found in southeastern New York. Historic towns line the riverbanks. Many of the grand old mansions in these towns have been restored, offering a look back into what life was like in the early years of Dutch and English settlement. Along the Hudson, just 50 miles north of New York City, is the United States Military Academy at West Point. The academy has been training Army cadets since 1802 and is still an operational fort. Its graduates include Ulysses S. Grant and Robert E. Lee as well as Dwight D. Eisenhower and George S. Patton. West Point is also one of the major tourist attractions in New York.[2]

A trip straight down the Hudson Valley ends right in the heart of a region that is taken up by one city—*New York City*. From there, it is just a short trip to *Long Island*, the state's easternmost point. It is 118 miles long and from 3 to 20 miles wide. The New York City boroughs of Brooklyn and Queens occupy the western tip of the island. The rest of the island is home to suburbs, farms, and coastal towns that become seaside resorts in the summer. Bordered to the north by Long Island Sound and the south by the Atlantic Ocean, Long Island is also home to a large commercial and sport fishing industry.

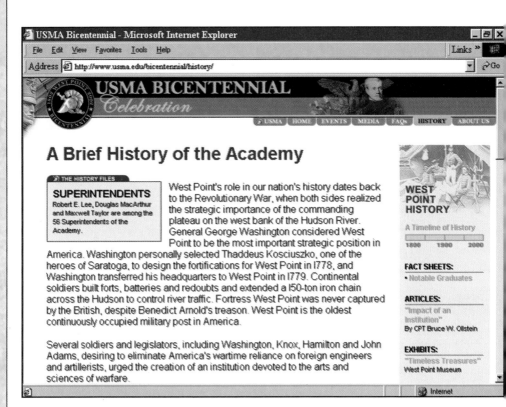

USMA Bicentennial - Microsoft Internet Explorer

File   Edit   View   Favorites   Tools   Help

Links »

Address http://www.usma.edu/bicentennial/history/

USMA BICENTENNIAL
Celebration

USMA   HOME   EVENTS   MEDIA   FAQs   **HISTORY**   ABOUT US

A Brief History of the Academy

THE HISTORY FILES

SUPERINTENDENTS
Robert E. Lee, Douglas MacArthur and Maxwell Taylor are among the 56 Superintendents of the Academy.

West Point's role in our nation's history dates back to the Revolutionary War, when both sides realized the strategic importance of the commanding plateau on the west bank of the Hudson River. General George Washington considered West Point to be the most important strategic position in America. Washington personally selected Thaddeus Kosciuszko, one of the heroes of Saratoga, to design the fortifications for West Point in 1778, and Washington transferred his headquarters to West Point in 1779. Continental soldiers built forts, batteries and redoubts and extended a 150-ton iron chain across the Hudson to control river traffic. Fortress West Point was never captured by the British, despite Benedict Arnold's treason. West Point is the oldest continuously occupied military post in America.

Several soldiers and legislators, including Washington, Knox, Hamilton and John Adams, desiring to eliminate America's wartime reliance on foreign engineers and artillerists, urged the creation of an institution devoted to the arts and sciences of warfare.

WEST POINT HISTORY
A Timeline of History
1800   1900   2000

FACT SHEETS:
• Notable Graduates

ARTICLES:
"Impact of an Institution"
By CPT Bruce W. Ollstein

EXHIBITS:
"Timeless Treasures"
West Point Museum

Internet

▲ *Situated on the banks of the Hudson River, the United States Military Academy at West Point is the oldest continuously operating fort in the United States as well as an institution of higher learning. It is one of the most popular tourist destinations in New York State.*

The land northwest of the Hudson Valley becomes the rolling *Catskills* region. Part of the Appalachian mountain system, the Catskill Mountains get their name from the Dutch word *Kaaterskill*, which translates in English to "wildcat creek." With more than 6,000 square miles of mountains and forests and six major river systems, the region is a destination for those who like hiking, fishing, and camping. It is also a land of orchards and vineyards. The Catskills region was also known for years as "the playground for New York City" because of its many large resorts that catered to urban Jewish New Yorkers.[3]

Farther northwest is the *Central-Leatherstocking* region. The name comes from James Fenimore Cooper's *Leatherstocking Tales,* five novels about Natty Bumpo and his life in the wilderness.[4] This is dairy and farming country. It is also home to Howe Caverns, in Schoharie County. The caverns are underground limestone caves that feature unusual rock formations. Visitors to the caverns can take a gondola-type boat ride on the "mirror perfect" Lake of Venus.

Directly west is a huge area called the *Finger Lakes.* The region is so-named because, on a map, Lakes Seneca, Cayuga, Owasco, and others look like fingers of water

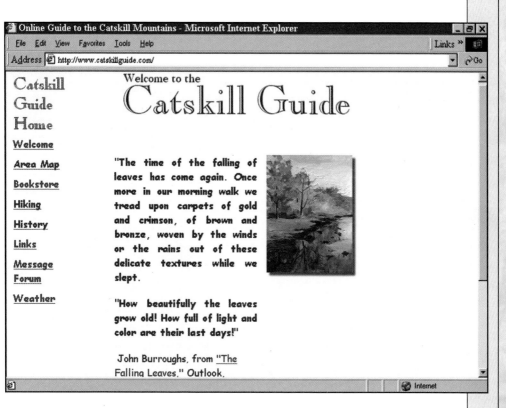

Skiing, hiking, and camping are just some of the outdoor pleasures to be found in the Catskill Mountains in northeastern New York.

running up and down. This is the state's premier wine country. There is auto racing at the Watkins Glen International Race Track and outdoor glass blowing at the famous Museum of Glass in Corning. Syracuse and Rochester, two of the state's largest cities, are in this region.

The two most western regions of New York are *Chautauqua-Allegheny* in the southwest and *Greater Niagara* in the northwest. Chautauqua-Allegheny is a world away from New York City's hustle and bustle. Here are colorful, elaborate old homes living through the centuries in Victorian splendor. There is also the 6,500-acre Allegheny State Park with its beautiful scenery and wildlife viewing.

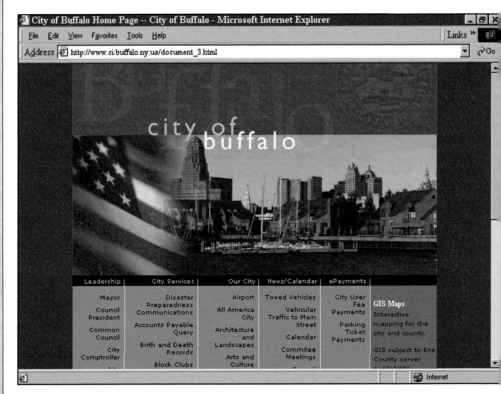

Buffalo is the second largest city in New York, with a population of nearly 300,000.

Greater Niagara's main attraction is its famous natural wonder—Niagara Falls. Niagara Falls is actually two falls, separated by Goat Island. The larger part, called Horseshoe Falls, 170 feet high and about 2,500 feet across, is on the Canadian side. The smaller, the American Falls, is 180 feet high and about 1,100 feet across.[5] Many visitors to the falls enjoy the view from the *Maid of the Mist*. This Niagara boat ride has been showing off the falls for more than 150 years. Before skydiving and bungee jumping became popular in the 1990s, Niagara Falls had its own daredevils. People still occasionally try to ride down the falls in a barrel or walk above them on a tightrope!

The Greater Niagara region is also home to the city of Buffalo, which is situated on the eastern shore of Lake Erie and the Buffalo and Niagara Rivers. The state's second largest city, Buffalo is a leading commercial and industrial port. The Peace Bridge, completed in 1927, connects the city with Fort Erie, Ontario. Since Buffalo borders Canada, the city is often chosen as the site of meetings between that country and the United States.

Climate

New York's varied geography produces a varied climate. When the Dutch settled the land that is today the island of Manhattan, they were not pleased with the weather. Since Manhattan lies at the same latitude as countries in Europe's warm Mediterranean region, the Dutch were rather amazed to discover cold winters with snow in southern New York.

New York has a temperate climate, although there are great differences in temperature and precipitation between New York City, for instance, and cities to the northwest, such as Buffalo. The average January temperature

in Buffalo is 24°F and in New York City, 32°F. The average July temperature in Buffalo is 71°F and in New York City, 76°F.[6]

The state's average yearly precipitation (rain, snow, and other forms of moisture) ranges from 32 to 58 inches. The Adirondacks, Catskills, and Long Island receive the greatest amount of precipitation in the form of rain. The city of Buffalo and other areas bordered by the Great Lakes receive abundant snowfall.

▲ *Niagara Falls.*

Economy

Many kinds of businesses make the state of New York run. Most of the state's jobs are in the service sector, which includes thousands of hotels, motels, restaurants, and other related businesses. Although manufacturing has declined from the days when it was New York's primary industry, it is still important and employs about one fifth of the state's workers.

▶ Making, Moving, Trading

The city of Rochester is known for its photographic and optical equipment industries. Syracuse specializes in producing metals, machinery, and paper products. Binghamton was the first home of the International Business Machine Corporation, better known as IBM. The company still employs many area residents in the manufacture of computers and business machines. The Utica-Rome metropolitan region manufactures machinery, and the Albany-Troy-Schenectady metropolitan region is home to paper manufacturers.

Transportation is also big business in New York and has been so for much of the state's history. The New York State Barge Canal System, completed in 1918, is a large inland waterway that connects some of the state's largest cities. Once used to ship many kinds of manufactured goods, it is used today mainly for moving petroleum products. The state's railway system is an important handler of freight. Much of that freight goes out of the Port

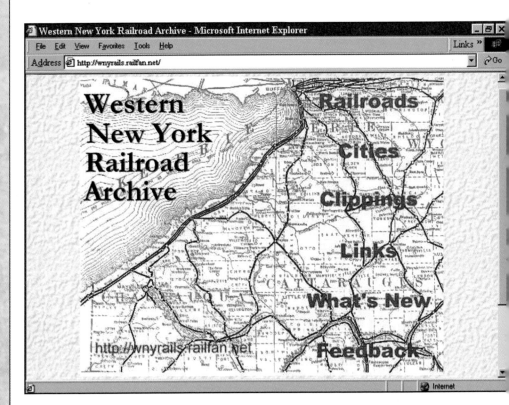

Western New York Railroad Archive - Microsoft Internet Explorer

File   Edit   View   Favorites   Tools   Help

Links »

Address   http://wnyrails.railfan.net/

Western
New York
Railroad
Archive

Railroads

Cities

Clippings

Links

What's New

Feedback

http://wnyrails.railfan.net

▲ *The railroad has played an important part in the history of New York. In the year 1900, the western part of the state was served by seven major railroads, transporting people and goods from Buffalo to New York City.*

of New York/New Jersey, the largest port system on the East Coast of North America.[1] The ports in this metropolitan region handle about one tenth of the nation's imported goods. The state's highway system helps to move goods and people, too, as do the airports in all of the major and some of the smaller New York cities. Albany, Buffalo, Syracuse, and Rochester all have airports. The New York-New Jersey metropolitan region's bridges, tunnels, airports, and terminals are administered by the Port Authority of New York and New Jersey, an agency of both states. The three main airports that serve the area are John F. Kennedy

International, La Guardia, and Newark International (in New Jersey).

Finance, insurance, and real estate operations are mainly concentrated in and around New York City. The financial district, home to stock exchanges and other financial businesses, is situated on and around Wall Street, in lower Manhattan. Wall Street is less than a mile long. Around 1653, a wall was built on the site to protect the Dutch settlers from invaders. The invaders never came, and the English tore down the wall in 1699. The New York Stock Exchange moved onto the site in the nineteenth century. After that, "Wall Street" became synonymous with the stock market itself.

▶ Fashion, Farming, Tourism, and Sports

New York City is also a major international center of the fashion and clothing industry. Several blocks on the west side of midtown are known as the garment district. In fact, Seventh Avenue between 38th and 40th Streets has come to be known as "Fashion Avenue." Visitors walking through the garment district during business hours often dodge carts and racks filled with the

The heart of the financial ▶ district, Wall Street is one of two New York streets (Broadway is the other) whose names have come to symbolize entire industries.

latest styles of clothing. Printing, publishing, advertising, and entertainment are also major businesses in the city.

Although farming is not one of the top industries in the state, dairy farming accounts for more than half the total farm income. Apples produced by the state's many orchards are one of New York's leading crops. Vineyards in the Finger Lakes region and Long Island have made the state well known for its wines. Fruit and vegetable farms are important, too. And New York competes with Vermont in the production of maple sugar.

Tourism is very big business. Millions of tourists visit the state each year from the rest of the country and abroad. More than 30 million tourists yearly visit New York City alone.[2] The United Nations and live theater are two of the main attractions in the city. One of the city's first theaters was built on Broadway in the 1730s. This street, originally an American Indian trail, runs the entire length of Manhattan, and like Wall Street, has come to symbolize an entire industry. Today, however, the main theater district is located on the side streets off Broadway, from about Times Square, at 42nd Street, to 49th Street. Most Americans know Times Square as the place where the ball drops every New Year's Eve. Broadway is also known as the Great White Way because of the hundreds of electric signs that advertise the district. In addition to the stage productions on Broadway, there are productions that have come to be known as Off-Broadway and Off-Off Broadway. In these small theaters, usually downtown or on the far east and west sides, the shows may be a little more experimental and the price of tickets a little less expensive.

Professional sports are also important to New York's economy. New York has three professional football teams: the New York Giants and the New York Jets, which play

▲ *In the Bronx, Yankee Stadium, "the house that Ruth built," is home to the world-famous New York Yankees baseball team.*

their games at Giants Stadium in East Rutherford, New Jersey, and the Buffalo Bills, which play in Ralph Wilson Stadium, in Orchard Park, a suburb of Buffalo. In baseball, the New York Yankees play at Yankee Stadium in the Bronx, and the Mets at Shea Stadium in Queens. The New York Knickerbockers in basketball and the New York Rangers in hockey both make Madison Square Garden, in New York City, their home. The state's other two professional hockey teams are the New York Islanders, who skate in Uniondale, on Long Island, and the Buffalo Sabres. The state is also home to professional soccer, lacrosse, and women's basketball teams.

Chapter 4

Government

New York's first constitution was adopted in 1777. Its present constitution was adopted in 1894 and has been amended many times since. The state's highest official is the governor, who is elected to a four-year term and may be reelected. Other elected state officials are the lieutenant governor, the attorney general, and the comptroller. The legislature is made up of two houses: the Senate, with sixty-one members, and the Assembly, with one hundred fifty members. Members of both houses serve two-year terms. New York has two United States senators and thirty-one representatives. In the national election of 2000, New York scored a historic first. Hillary Rodham Clinton, wife of then-incumbent president Bill Clinton, was elected a senator from New York. She became the first First Lady in the country's history to be elected to political office.

New York's court system divides the state into twelve districts. Each has several elected judges. Together they form the state supreme court. The highest court in the state is the court of appeals. Seven judges serve on it. They are appointed by the governor, with the Senate's approval, to fourteen-year terms.

Most of the state's urban areas are governed by a mayor and council. New York City's council includes a president, comptroller in charge of finances, and presidents of each of the five boroughs that make up the city. New York City's government is older than the government of the United States. The Dutch set up the first local government in 1653 in what was then New Amsterdam.

▶ Albany, the State Capital

The capital of New York is Albany. One of the nation's oldest cities, Albany is situated on the west bank of the Hudson River in Albany County, 143 miles north of New York City. Explorer Henry Hudson first saw the area on his 1609 voyage to the New World. By 1614, the Dutch had built a fur-trading post there. Ten years later, it became a permanent settlement, named "Fort Orange" for the royal family of the Netherlands. In 1652, the colony's governor, Peter Stuyvesant, renamed the settlement around Fort Orange "Beverwyck." When the English took over in

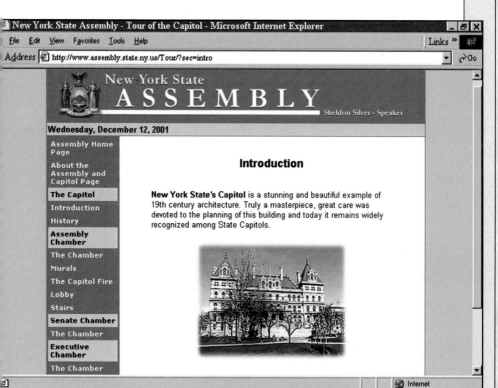

The State Capitol, in Albany, is the home of New York's state government. The Capitol building, constructed in the nineteenth century, is remarkable for its combination of different architectural styles.

1664, it was renamed "Albany." The name honors King James II, who was the Duke of York and of Albany.

Albany was chosen as the state capital in 1797. When the Erie Canal opened, in 1825, Albany also became linked to Lake Erie and the state's interior. With the coming of the railroad, in 1831, the city became a railroad hub for the Great Lakes. Albany's Dutch beginnings can be seen in many examples of Dutch architecture to be found in the city. Historic Cherry Hill, today a museum, was once the grand home of the Van Rensselaer family. A popular tourist stop is Fort Crailo, built about 1700. It is there that Richard Shuckburgh is said to have written the lyrics to the song "Yankee Doodle Dandy." Albany is also a rich cultural center. It is the site of the New York State Museum, the New York State Library and Archives, and the Albany Institute of History and Art.

Albany, however, is mainly about government. The focal point of the city is Empire State Plaza. This vast modern complex houses government offices as well as cultural and convention facilities. The plaza sits on ninety-eight acres of land and connects eleven buildings to the state Capitol. The plaza also houses the Governor Nelson A. Rockefeller Empire State Plaza Art Collection, an impressive collection of modern American art. Nelson Rockefeller was the governor of New York from 1959 to 1973 and the vice president of the United States from 1974 to 1977.

▶ Party Politics

In New York politics, the Republican Party is usually strong upstate and on Long Island, while the Democratic Party is strong in New York City. Since 1920, however, the Big Apple has also had Republican mayors. A pull between the rest of the state and the city has long caused friction between the two sides during election time. And because the population of the New York City metropolitan area is close to half the population of the entire state, a strong showing in the city can often swing an election. That adds to the love-hate relationship between upstate New York and New York City. New Yorkers who live outside of New York City tend to resent the focus and attention paid to the city, as though nothing else in the state exists. The people of New York City, on the other hand, tend to think that nothing else *does* exist.

Education

New York State has one of the broadest educational systems in the country. The University of the State of New York, established in 1784, is not a university in the common sense of the term, but an agency. It is governed by a sixteen-member board of regents, who are elected to seven-year terms by the state legislature. The board sets the state's educational standards, distributes funds, and awards scholarships, among other things. In 1948, teachers colleges, two-year colleges, and all other institutions of higher learning were placed into the State University of New York (SUNY) system. Major university centers are located at Stony Brook, Albany, Binghamton, and Buffalo. The City University of New York (CUNY) is supported by both the state and New York City and is made up of such institutions as City College, Brooklyn College, and Queens College. There are also more than two hundred private institutions of higher learning in the state, including Syracuse University, Colgate University, Cornell University, and Columbia University. Founded in 1754 as King's College, Columbia is the oldest university in the state.

Chapter 5

History

In the year 1609, Henry Hudson sailed his ship the *Half Moon* up the river that is now named for him. Hudson, an English explorer working for the Dutch East India Company, was overjoyed because he thought that he had found the Northwest Passage. This was a long-searched-for route across the American continent to the Pacific Ocean. However, after traveling upstream for about 150 miles,

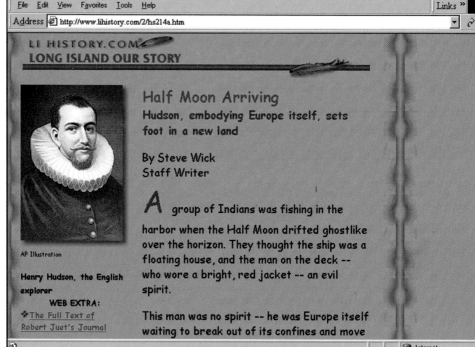

Half Moon Arriving - Microsoft Internet Explorer

File   Edit   View   Favorites   Tools   Help   Links »

Address http://www.lihistory.com/2/hs214a.htm

LI HISTORY.COM
LONG ISLAND OUR STORY

Half Moon Arriving
Hudson, embodying Europe itself, sets foot in a new land

By Steve Wick
Staff Writer

A group of Indians was fishing in the harbor when the Half Moon drifted ghostlike over the horizon. They thought the ship was a floating house, and the man on the deck -- who wore a bright, red jacket -- an evil spirit.

This man was no spirit -- he was Europe itself waiting to break out of its confines and move

AP Illustration

Henry Hudson, the English explorer

WEB EXTRA:
❖The Full Text of Robert Juet's Journal

Internet

In 1609, sailing for the Dutch East India Company, the explorer Henry Hudson sailed up the river that now bears his name.

nearly to what is today Albany, Hudson changed his mind. It was obvious the river did not lead to the Pacific.

Early Explorers, Earlier Inhabitants

Henry Hudson was not the first person to see the Hudson River, and not even the first European. Giovanni da Verrazano of Florence, sailing for France, was most likely the first European explorer to land in New York. Verrazano explored New York Bay and saw the river in 1524. The Verrazano-Narrows Bridge, which connects the boroughs of Brooklyn and Staten Island and is the world's longest suspension bridge, is named for him.

The Hudson River might well be called the Iroquois or the Algonquian. The members of these two American Indian groups were early inhabitants of the land surrounding the Hudson, and beyond. The Algonquian, which included the Mahican, the Delaware, and the Wappinger tribes, lived chiefly in the Hudson Valley and north to Lake Champlain. The Iroquois lived mainly in the western and central parts of New York. The Iroquois included the Mohawk, Oneida, Onondaga, Cayuga, and Seneca tribes. In about 1570, these tribes came together to from the Iroquois Confederacy, also called the League of the Five Nations. The confederacy functioned as a remarkably democratic group. They hoped to keep peace by becoming a strong and fearsome band that was united against its enemies. In the early 1700s, the Tuscarora, an Iroquoian tribe that migrated to New York from the South, joined the confederacy. The group's name then became the League of the Six Nations.

The league worked for a time against other American Indian tribes. It did not work for long, though, against invading European explorers and settlers. However, the Six

Nations' influence can still be seen in the many Indian place names that are to be found throughout the state. When the Dutch and then the English settled parts of New York, they usually just adopted American Indian names as their own, such as Poughkeepsie, Schenectady, and hundreds of others.

▶ From New Amsterdam to New York

In 1624, the Dutch West India Company established the colony of New Netherland in what is today New York. Then about forty Dutch colonists landed on Manhattan

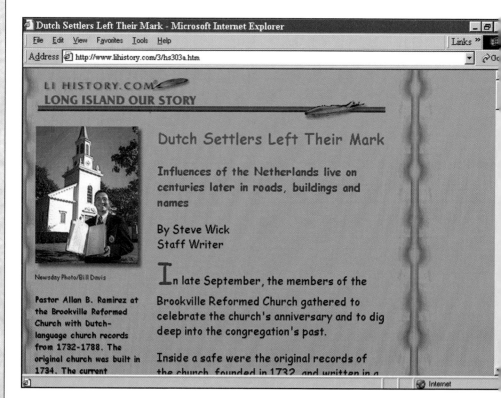

New York was settled in the seventeenth century by Dutch immigrants, who called the colony "New Netherland." New York's Dutch heritage can be found in the many examples of Dutch architecture that remain and in the place names whose origins are Dutch.

Island and set up the "sailor's town" of New Amsterdam. It is said that the colony's governor, Peter Minuit, paid the American Indians who lived in the area the equivalent of twenty-four dollars for the land. New Amsterdam would later became New York City. However, the settlement of New Amsterdam never amounted to much under Dutch rule. In fact, a visiting missionary in 1643 said so many different people were going there, speaking so many tongues, that it caused "our chief unhappyness" of "too great a mixture" of different races and religions.[1] More than 350 years later, most people think that this same diversity is one of the city's great virtues.

The English were also attracted to New Amsterdam. In 1664, a small English fleet sailed into the harbor and declared ownership. The colony's governor, Peter Stuyvesant, was without any resources to defend New Amsterdam, so he surrendered without a fight. His government back home did not seem to care who owned the town. At the time the Netherlands was more interested in trade than colonies, and was involved in a war with England. So, without a shot fired, New Amsterdam became British and was renamed New York, after the Duke of York, later King James II. Except for a brief two-year period (1673–74) when the Dutch recaptured New York, it remained in the hands of the British until the end of the Revolutionary War. The British government, however, did not seem that much more interested in its new land than the Dutch had been. There was no effort to force, or even encourage, the Dutch colonists to learn English. As a result, Dutch customs and language persisted for the next two hundred years all along the Hudson Valley. Many traces of Dutch heritage remain today.

New York at War

Until well into the eighteenth century, about two thirds of the colony's population lived around the growing city of New York. There was also little settlement beyond Albany because the English and French were fighting the French and Indian War (1754–63) in the northern and central parts of New York. When the war ended, England controlled all of New York. Gradually, settlers began moving in from New England.

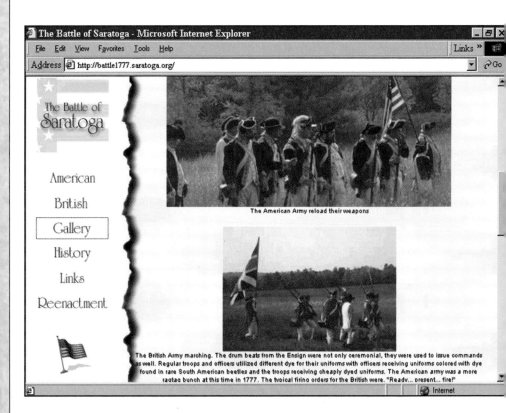

The American Army reload their weapons

The British Army marching. The drum beats from the Ensign were not only ceremonial, they were used to issue commands as well. Regular troops and officers utilized different dye for their uniforms with officers receiving uniforms colored with dye found in rare South American beetles and the troops receiving cheaply dyed uniforms. The American army was a more ragtag bunch at this time in 1777. The typical firing orders for the British were. "Ready... present... fire!"

In northeastern New York, the small resort town of Saratoga is known today for horse racing. But it was the site more than two hundred years ago of one of the most pivotal battles of the Revolutionary War. The Continental Army's victories over the British at Saratoga helped convince the French to aid the American cause.

When the American Revolution began in 1775, New York had a population of about 163,000. It was the seventh largest of the thirteen colonies. Although some of the colonists of New York did not like the idea of splitting from Great Britain, many others served in the Continental Army. New York played a pivotal role in the war, even though New York City was captured by the British and remained in their hands until the war's end. Nearly one third of all the battles of the Revolution took place on New York soil. The American victories at Saratoga proved to be a turning point in the Revolution, since they convinced the French to offer aid to the Americans.[2] New York would also be a battleground during the War of 1812, which was fought mostly along the state's northern border with Canada.

Growth and Expansion

After the Revolutionary War, New York sent delegates to the Constitutional Convention, in Philadelphia. The New York delegates, including Alexander Hamilton, favored a strong central government. In 1788, New York became the eleventh state to ratify the Constitution. And from 1785 to 1790, New York City served as the nation's capital. It was here in 1789 that George Washington was inaugurated the first president of the United States.

The 1800 census marked New York as the second largest state in the Union, behind only Virginia. When the Erie Canal opened in 1825, New York became the gateway to the west from the Atlantic coast. Over the next decades, the state grew in area and population. There was also growth in manufacturing and in transportation with the construction of rail lines that paralleled the canal route. Cities along the canal, such as Buffalo, Rome, Utica, Syracuse, and Schenectady, grew and prospered. In the

NYC 100: Virtue Over Vice, but Barely - Microsoft Internet Explorer

File   Edit   View   Favorites   Tools   Help   Links »

Address http://www.nytimes.com/specials/nyc100/nyc100-1-quinn.html

1899

The "Boulevard" becomes Broadway above 59th Street.

City has 43 newpapers; 23 are in English.

Bronx Zoo, Brooklyn Children's Museum open.

30-story Park Row building is world's tallest.

1900

The International Ladies Garment Workers Union is formed

United Press International

THE LOWER EAST SIDE, pictured here about 1900, teemed with immigrants. By decade's end, a million people a year were arriving at Ellis Island; a quarter stayed in New York.

In the sprawling slums of New York, the so-called other half lived as it always had, mostly hand to mouth. The tenement districts, concentrated near the Manhattan and Brooklyn shorelines, were home to notoriously squalid and overcrowded conditions, a source of misery to those who endured them and a concern to those who studied them.

Activists like Lillian Wald tried to relieve the physical suffering of the immigrant poor and help them find means of escape. Others were increasingly alarmed by the increasing presence of foreigners. In 1902, almost 500,000 immigrants landed at Ellis Island. By the end of

Done   Internet

The population of New York City by 1860 made it the largest city in the United States. The newly arrived immigrants to America who came from Ireland and Germany contributed to much of that growth.

nineteenth century, New York also led the way in various reforms, banning slavery in 1827 and holding the first women's rights convention, in Seneca Falls in 1848.

The Immigrant Waves

As the state was growing, so was New York City. It was the largest city in the nation by 1860. And the population was also becoming more diverse as waves of Irish and German immigrants fled famine and revolution in Europe, beginning in the 1840s. Their first stop in America was usually New York City. New York had also become the country's financial capital. The city, with its size and power, was often at odds with the rest of the state, which was far more rural and conservative. That conflict exists to some extent today.

With the start of the Civil War, in 1861, New York would once again send its sons into battle. The state was a strong supporter of the preservation of the Union, and many New Yorkers served in the Civil War. One third of all the soldiers killed in the First Battle of Bull Run were from New York.

In the latter part of the nineteenth century into the first three decades of the twentieth, a second wave of

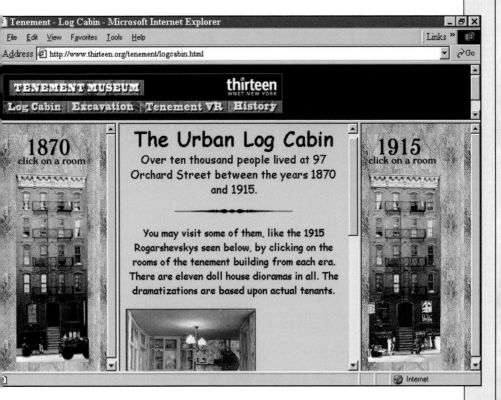

Many immigrants lived in New York City's tenements. The Tenement Museum in the city offers a glimpse of what tenement life in the late 1800s and early 1900s was like.

immigration poured into the city and the state. These people, from Ireland, Italy, and Eastern Europe, arrived at Ellis Island, in New York Harbor. New York's population again surged. The labor that the immigrants provided allowed manufacturing to continue its growth into the twentieth century, although working conditions were often horrible for the poorest laborers. The growth of labor unions and especially Theodore Roosevelt's support for them, in the early part of the twentieth century, brought improvements in working conditions. The Great Depression, which started in 1929, took a great toll on New Yorkers, especially those in urban areas.

Despite the setbacks during the Depression, the state continued to expand in all industrial areas until after World War II. The state's manufacturing base has declined ever since. And with the loss of jobs, many of the old manufacturing cities, like Buffalo and Rochester, saw residents move out, either to the suburbs or out of state. The 1970s were a particularly hard time for the state and the city, which came close to bankruptcy by the middle of the decade. But in the 1980s and 1990s, the economy in New York, like that in the rest of the country, rebounded.

▶ A Second "Day That Will Live in Infamy"

And then on September 11, 2001, New York City became the site of the worst terrorist attack in U.S. history. On that clear, sunlit morning, as people were just beginning their workday, having breakfast, or going to school, terrorists hijacked four American commercial jetliners. They crashed two of them into the twin towers of the World Trade Center, in lower Manhattan. At 110 stories high, the towers were the city's tallest buildings and a fixture of the Manhattan skyline. When they were completed, in 1973,

This photograph taken before September 11, 2001, highlights the twin towers of the World Trade Center. The towers, at 110 stories, were the city's tallest buildings and a majestic part of the city skyline.

it was thought that they could withstand the impact of a plane crash. But they could not withstand the explosion that came when two planes, fully loaded with fuel, were flown straight into them.

All those aboard the planes were killed. More than 2,500 people working in the Trade Center were killed. More than 450 of the courageous police officers, firefighters, and emergency services workers who rushed to the scene lost their lives trying to rescue them. The world watched in horror as the towers, once the world's tallest buildings, collapsed. But the attack on New York City was not the only one that morning. The third hijacked plane attacked the Pentagon, outside Washington, D.C., killing nearly 200 people. The fourth hijacked plane crashed in a field in western

Emergency workers are shown amid the devastation that was once the World Trade Center. After the September 11, 2001, attacks, the site became known as Ground Zero. More than 3,000 people lost their lives that day in lower Manhattan.

Pennsylvania, its intended target unknown. In all, nearly 4,000 people were killed by the terrorist attacks of September 11.

People around the world were affected by the events of that day, as all airline travel in and out of the United States was halted and the stock market remained closed for the rest of that week. And people across America were shocked by a terrorist attack of that magnitude happening on American soil.

▶ Excelsior

The amount of money it will take to clear the site where the towers once stood is enormous. The losses in revenue to New York City and New York State are calculated to be in the billions of dollars. The loss of life and the loss of innocence cannot be measured. But what the terrorists never took into account was the spirit and resolve of the people of New York. That spirit, toughness, and courage would see the city through its worst day. In the hours, days, and months following September 11, New Yorkers have continued to show their strength and their heart. And though none who were there that day can ever forget its horror, New Yorkers seem determined to look to the future. In that, they are truly embodying the spirit of the state motto, *Excelsior*, "Ever Upward."

Chapter Notes

Chapter 1. The State of New York

1. Niagara County Tourism Department, "Welcome to Niagara—USA.com," *Niagara USA—The Official Website of Niagara County Tourism,* n.d., <http://www.niagara-usa.com/pages/play2htm> (December 13, 2001).

2. Lincoln Center for the Performing Arts, *Home page,* n.d., <http://www.lincolncenter.org/default.asp> (December 13, 2001).

Chapter 2. Land and Climate

1. Brunner, Borgna, ed., *The Time Almanac 2002* (Boston: Information Please, 2001), p. 162.

2. The United States Military Academy, "USMA Visitors Center," *The United States Military Academy,* December 4, 2001, <http://www.usma.edu/PublicAffairs/vic.htm> (December 13, 2001).

3. Brown, Phil, "Catskill Culture: The Rise and Fall of a Jewish Resort Area Seen Through Personal Narrative and Ethnography," excerpted in *The Catskills Institute,* n.d., <http://www.brown.edu/Research/Catskills_Institute/culture.html> (December 13, 2001).

4. James Fenimore Cooper, *The Pioneers* (New York: Charles Wiley, 1823), *The Last of the Mohicans* (Philadelphia: Lea, 1826), *The Prairie* (Philadelphia: Carey, Lea, and Carey, 1827), *The Pathfinder* (Philadelphia: Lea and Blanchard, 1840), *The Deerslayer* (Philadelphia: Lea and Blanchard, 1841).

5. HistoryChannel.com, "Niagara: The Story of the Falls," *The HistoryChannel.com,* n.d., <http://www.historychannel.com/exhibits/niagara/snapshots.html> (December 13, 2001).

6. Brunner, p. 606.

Chapter 3. Economy

1. "The Port of New York/New Jersey," *The Port Authority of New York and New Jersey,* n.d., <http://www.panynj.gov/commerce/marframe.htm> (December 13, 2001).

2. New York City Convention and Visitors Bureau, "Fun Facts," *New York City and Company,* n.d., <http://www.nycvisit.com/fun_facts.html> (December 13, 2001).

Chapter 5. History

1. Marshall B. Davidson, *New York: A Pictorial History* (New York: Scribner's, 1997), p. 5.

2. PBS Online, "Burgoyne Surrenders at Saratoga," *Liberty! Chronicle of the Revolution,* n.d., <http://www.pbs.org/ktca/liberty/chronicle/episode4.html> (December 13, 2001).

Further Reading

Davidson, Marshall B. *New York: A Pictorial History*. New York: Scribner's, 1997.

Diamonstein, Barbaralee. *Landmarks: Eighteen Wonders of the New York World*. New York: Harry N. Abrams, 1992.

Heinrichs, Ann, and R. Conrad Stein. *New York*. Danbury, Conn.: Children's Press, 1999.

Jackson, Kenneth T., ed. *The Encyclopedia of New York City*. New Haven, Conn.: Yale University Press, 1995.

Janvier, Thomas A. *In Old New York: A Classic History of New York City*. New York: St. Martin's Press, 2000.

Kavanaugh, James. *The Nature of New York City*. Blaine, Wash.: Wateford Press, 1997.

Sanford, William R. *The Revolutionary War Soldier at Saratoga*. Mankato, Minn.: Capstone Press, 1991.

Schomp, Virginia. *Celebrate the States: New York*. Tarrytown, N.Y.: Marshall Cavendish Corporation, 1996.

Slovey, Christine. *Harlem Renaissance*. Farmington Hills, Mich.: Gale Group, 2001.

Stewart, Frances T. *City Grows Up: New York*. New York: Smithmark Publishers, 1991.

Welsbacher, Anne. *New York*. Edina, Minn.: ABDO Publishing Company, 1998.

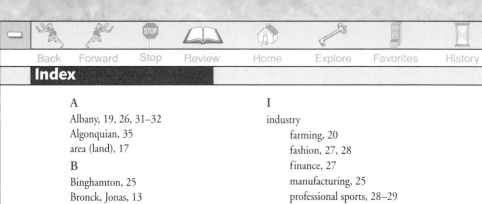